SHOCKWAVE
SOCIAL STUDIES

Liberty

Blessing or Burden?

PETER REES

children's press®
An imprint of Scholastic Inc.
NEW YORK • TORONTO • LONDON • AUCKLAND • SYDNEY
MEXICO CITY • NEW DELHI • HONG KONG
DANBURY, CONNECTICUT

Library of Congress Cataloging-in-Publication Data

Rees, Peter, 1966-
Liberty : blessing or burden? / by Peter Rees.
p. cm. -- (Shockwave)
Includes index.

ISBN-10: 0-531-17760-2 (lib. bdg.)
ISBN-13: 978-0-531-17760-0 (lib. bdg.)
ISBN-10: 0-531-15494-7 (pbk.)
ISBN-13: 978-0-531-15494-6 (pbk.)

1. Liberty--Juvenile literature. 2. Civil rights--Juvenile literature.
3. Democracy--Juvenile literature. 4. Responsibility--Juvenile literature.
5. Political science--Juvenile literature. I. Title. II. Series.

JC585.R434 2008
323.44--dc22
2007010061

Published in 2008 by Children's Press, an imprint of Scholastic Inc.,
557 Broadway, New York, New York 10012
www.scholastic.com

08 09 10 11 12 13 14 15 16 17
10 9 8 7 6 5 4 3 2 1

Printed in China through Colorcraft Ltd., Hong Kong

Author: Peter Rees
Editors: Lynette Evans and Jeannie Hutchins
Designer: Emma Alsweiler
Photo Researchers: Jamshed Mistry and Sarah Matthewson

Photographs by: aapimage.com/AP (Statue of Liberty, p. 15); **Getty Images** (courtroom,
p. 20; p. 22; pp. 26–27); **Jennifer and Brian Lupton** (girl, p. 6; pro and con students,
pp. 30–31); **Photolibrary** (p. 5; Velvet Revolution, p. 11; Nelson Mandela, p. 25; p. 28;
jeans shopping, pp. 30–31); **Richard Saunders** (p. 14); **TopFoto/www.stockcentral.co.nz**
(Cyrus Cylinder, p. 9); **Tranz/Corbis** (cover; p. 8; The Code of Hammurabi, p. 9; p. 10;
anti-globalization protest, pp. 10–11; p. 13; Liberty Bell, p. 15; pp. 16–19; p. 21;
pp. 23–24; police and protester, p. 25)

The publisher would like to thank Seth Janssen (p. 30) and Onyinyechukwu Agbo (p. 31)

All illustrations and other photographs © Weldon Owen Education Inc.

CONTENTS

democracy (*di MOK ruh see*) a way of governing a country in which the people choose their leaders in elections

equality (*i KWOL uh tee*) the same rights for everyone

injustice (*in JUHSS tiss*) unfairness

liberty (*LIB ur tee*) freedom

prejudice (*PREJ uh diss*) hatred or unfair treatment that comes from having fixed opinions about some groups of people

protest a demonstration or statement against something, as in a protest against war

responsibility (*ri spon suh BIL uh tee*) a duty or a job

revolution (*rev uh LOO shuhn*) an uprising by the people of a country that changes the way in which the country is governed

For easy reference, see Wordmark on back flap.
For additional vocabulary, see Glossary on page 32.

The prefix "in–" is one of several prefixes used to signal an opposite: *justice – injustice; appropriate – inappropriate*; and so on. Other prefixes are *im–, un–, dis–, ex–, ir–*.

Millions of people gather in towns and cities around the world to voice their opinions about current events.

When we are young, the world seems full of possibilities and freedom. Our parents assign us household chores, but mostly we are able to play and explore. As we grow older, we learn that freedom comes with **responsibilities**. Schools make rules. Governments make laws. Sometimes the rules and laws seem endless!

Josie is an imaginary sixteen-year-old in the United States. Sometimes she feels hemmed in by rules and restrictions. A typical day for Josie has a combination of freedoms and responsibilities. It's often difficult to tell them apart!

7:00 A.M.

The alarm goes off. Josie must get ready for school. In the United States, children must attend school until the age of sixteen.

Josie thinks that everyone would be happier if they could just do as they pleased. Do you agree with her?

8:15 A.M.

Josie waits at the light. Pedestrians, vehicles, and cyclists have to obey traffic laws, for safety and to keep roads running smoothly.

Some rules make sense. People are probably more comfortable when they know what is and what isn't allowed.

4:00 P.M.

Josie goes to her after-school job at a restaurant. She must follow strict rules about conduct and cleanliness. Her employer's freedom is limited too. He may not pay her less than the minimum wage.

Josie wouldn't dream of going to work in dirty clothes. Her employer might lose his workers if he paid them too little. What "restrictions" are just common sense?

12:00 noon

It's lunchtime. Josie's doctor has her on a low-fat diet for her health. This restricts her freedom of choice in foods.

7:30 P.M.

Josie wants to rent a DVD on her way home from work. Her mom won't allow her to get the movie she wants because it is rated R and marked "parental advisory."

The movie rating system restricts the freedom of young people to see some films. Is this a good thing?

9:00 A.M.

First period is science class. Josie must not talk in class. She must turn in her homework on time.

Some rules and restrictions are simply about being considerate of others, or holding up your end of an agreement.

9:30 P.M.

Josie would like to play with her cat, Rufus, but she has to finish some homework before bed. "I wish I were free like you," she says to Rufus.

Taking a Stand for Freedom

Most of us take our **liberty** for granted. Yet many of our freedoms are fairly new. Long ago, societies were organized into classes of people. Most were slaves or peasant farmers. They had to do as they were told. Even people higher up the social ladder were not truly free. They served a king or a queen, who could demand payments or force them to go to war.

Under these circumstances, liberty didn't come about by accident. It was demanded by those who didn't have it. Sometimes ordinary people had to fight for it. Some even died for it. History is full of stories of people, rich and poor, who were brave enough to stand up for their liberty.

SHOCKER

The **guillotine** was invented in Scotland. It was used during the French **Revolution** to make executions speedier and less painful.

Early Milestones of Liberty

There are many important milestones along the path to freedom. Here are some of the earliest ones.

King Hammurabi of Babylon (in present-day Iraq) wrote one of the earliest collections of laws. The Code of Hammurabi outlines freedoms for all people.

1750 B.C.

530 B.C.

Cyrus the Great ruled an empire that spread across the Middle East and beyond. He respected the rights of his **subjects**. The Cyrus Cylinder is one of the earliest declarations of human rights.

About 400 B.C.

The people of ancient Greece began a kind of government called **democracy**.

1215 A.D

A group of **barons** in England presented their king with a list of demands and made him sign. This list is called the Magna Carta. It was an early attempt to put basic liberties into law.

Riots and Revolutions

- In America in 1775, an eight-year-long battle for freedom led to the birth of a new nation – the United States. The Revolutionary War in America was an example to people around the world who later fought for their freedom.

- In the late 1700s, France was a **feudal** society. At the top, the king and nobles were well fed and wealthy. At the bottom, the starving peasants had to pay heavy taxes. They couldn't even eat rabbits, which were set aside for the nobles to hunt! In 1789, after the American colonists' successful battle for freedom, the French people rose up against their rulers. The motto for their revolution was "Liberty, **Equality**, Brotherhood!" They overthrew the king and formed a new government. The French Revolution was bloody, but it set France on a path toward democracy. Like the Revolutionary War, the French Revolution inspired other countries to stand up for their liberty.

Rebels and Revolutions

Revolutions are not necessarily events from the past, nor do they have to be violent. Marches, strikes, **protests**, and demonstrations can be peaceful yet powerful ways for people to gather to try to bring about change. Peaceful protesters can also use the Internet, e-mail, and cell phones to communicate their concerns. Today's "revolutionaries" are often ordinary people protesting about things such as the effects of global trade on jobs and the environment.

There are still uprisings in many parts of the world. Some are peaceful. Others are violent. Some are successful. Others do not lead to increased liberty for everyone. However, the struggle for political and economic liberty continues around the world.

Picture Power

This image of a Chinese protester stopping tanks was broadcast around the world on June 5, 1989. The man was taking part in a pro-democracy demonstration in Beijing's Tiananmen Square. The Chinese government crushed the protest, killing hundreds. It is not known whether the "tank man" survived.

Today, many people believe that the biggest threat to freedom is the spread of giant multinational businesses. They blame this "**globalization**" of trade for low wages, environmental damage, and other problems.

Other people want rich countries to stop demanding debt repayments from poor countries. They say the repayments keep the people in those countries in **poverty**.

Peaceful Protests

Beginning in the late 1980s, a series of mostly peaceful revolutions took place in Eastern Europe. Millions of protesters took to the streets in pursuit of civil and political freedoms. The revolution in Czechoslovakia was so smooth and peaceful, it became known as the Velvet Revolution. Other revolutions adopted **symbols** such as colors and flowers to get their message across.

Orange Revolution in Ukraine

11

Land of the Free?

The question mark in the heading makes me think that these pages may question the idea of freedom for all. Sometimes simple punctuation marks are really important!

We hold these truths to be self-evident, that all men are created equal, that they are endowed by their Creator with certain unalienable Rights, that among these are Life, Liberty and the pursuit of Happiness.

The Declaration of Independence was written by several leaders. It was completed on July 4, 1776, in the middle of the American colonies' fight for independence from British rule. The document marked the birth of the United States as a free and independent nation, though the war continued for seven more years. Its **ideals** of freedom and equality were unusual for their time. They were also difficult to live up to. Reality for most was not so clear-cut.

The Pilgrims

- The Pilgrims came to America to be free. Many had been treated unfairly at home because of their religion.
- In America, the Pilgrims dreamed of creating a society where everyone would be equal.
- When the Pilgrims arrived in America, they faced many hardships. To survive, personal freedom was often sacrificed for the good of the community.

The Africans

- Millions of Africans were brought to America in slave ships during the 1600s and 1700s.
- In America, Africans were sold as slaves to settlers and put to work on large farms and in cities. Nearly all African-American slaves spent a lifetime as another person's human property. They were not entitled to basic rights and freedoms.

The aim of America being a "land of the free" where life was fair and happy for all people was a noble idea. However, history shows us that there are many reasons why it did not turn out to be so for all who came to America.

- How could things have been made fair for all?

- What are some examples of people staying true to the ideals of freedom and equality?

- How could the new nation have grown while still respecting the rights of Native Americans?

The Native Americans

- Native Americans were the first people to live in this country. Many helped the Pilgrims survive in the new land. They taught the settlers how to farm and fish.

- During the 1800s, entire nations of Native Americans were forced off their land to allow settlers to expand west and settle new lands across America. Native groups were herded up and moved to reservations far away from their homes. Families were separated and many people died.

The Chinese

- In the 1860s, the United States government decided to expand railroad lines across the nation. This would be good for business and the economy.

- Thousands of Chinese workers were brought in to help build the Transcontinental Railroad. These **immigrants** were given little pay for backbreaking work. They suffered **discrimination** and had no way to protest.

13

Symbols of Liberty

In the days when **emigrants** came to the United States by sea, they were greeted in New York Harbor by a tall, female figure holding a flaming torch. In her left hand, she held a broken chain and shackle. Her name was *Liberty Enlightening the World*, but most knew her simply as the Statue of Liberty.

Most emigrants came to America in search of freedom – freedom from hunger, **prejudice**, **injustice**, or **tyranny**. The Statue of Liberty symbolized the liberty they hoped to find there. It remains a symbol of freedom to people around the world today.

The word *prejudice* is related to the term *prejudge*. *Pre* means "before." To prejudge someone or something means to form an opinion before considering all the facts. That opinion can be called a prejudice.

The Look of Liberty

Liberty was often shown as a woman in artworks and on coins. This idea comes from ancient Rome, where Libertas was the goddess of liberty. Liberty is shown here with a shield and an eagle. These are also symbols of the fight for freedom.

The Statue of Liberty was a gift from France to the United States. The statue was built in Paris and shipped to the United States in 214 crates. The completed statue was unveiled on October 28, 1886.

The Liberty Bell

The Liberty Bell is one of the most famous symbols of American freedom. It was rung on July 8, 1776, to celebrate the first public reading of the Declaration of Independence. The Liberty Bell weighs more than 2,000 pounds. Today, it hangs in Liberty Bell Center, Philadelphia.

What Are Civil Liberties?

Governments have to balance the need for laws with the individual's right to liberty. In democracies, there are some basic freedoms that laws cannot take away. These freedoms are called civil liberties. Some countries have a Bill of Rights that sets out the civil liberties of their citizens. In the United States, the Bill of Rights is part of the Constitution. Together, these rights protect people from the actions of bad governments. Watchdog groups make sure that governments don't make laws that take away people's civil liberties.

Some Important Civil Liberties

Freedom of Speech

This is the freedom to express your opinion without being punished.

Limitations: Freedom of speech does not give you the right to tell lies about other people, or to encourage others to commit crimes.

Freedom of Association

This is the freedom to choose the people with whom you spend your time. It includes the freedom to choose whom you marry and what organizations you join.

Limitations: On the other hand, an organization or business may not refuse to work with a person because of his or her race or religion.

Freedom of Religion

This is the freedom to follow any religion, or no religion.

Limitations: Some religious practices, such as polygamy (having more than one wife), are against the law.

Freedom of Assembly

This is the freedom to join or form any legal organization, such as a political party, trade union, or protest group.

Limitations: People may not belong to illegal organizations, such as terrorist groups.

Fights for Civil Rights

- Civil rights recognize that all people are entitled to be treated equally under the law.

- During the Civil Rights Movement in the 1960s, African Americans fought hard to gain equal opportunities. The 1964 Civil Rights Act and the 1965 Voting Rights Act were important victories in this battle.

The Right to Privacy

This is the right to conduct your private life without interference or intrusion from other people.

Limitations: Government agencies or the police are sometimes allowed to search or spy on criminal suspects.

Why Are There Limitations to Civil Liberties?

Imagine the danger and panic that could occur if a person falsely shouted "fire!" in a crowded theater. The right to free speech doesn't mean that people can say whatever they like. This is an example of why all civil liberties come with limitations and responsibilities. Rights must never be used to cause harm.

The Supreme Court hears many legal arguments over civil liberties in the United States. The Court is made up of nine senior judges. Their decisions help define the extent of civil liberties.

Right or Wrong?

1. In response to the September 11, 2001 terrorist attacks on United States targets, the United States government passed a set of laws called the Patriot Act. The Patriot Act gave the government broader powers to collect information about citizens. Many people argued that the Act went against people's civil liberties. Courts later declared parts of the Act unconstitutional.

What Do You Think **?**

1. What do you think about the Patriot Act?

2. Do you agree that groups have the right to express their views publicly, even if those views call for the denial of rights to other groups?

3. Do you think people should be allowed to wear whatever clothing or symbols they wish? Do you think that clothing or symbols to do with religion should be banned from places such as public schools?

2. The American Civil Liberties Union (ACLU) has defended the right of the Ku Klux Klan to assemble. However, the ACLU does not defend the right of groups to **violate** the civil rights of others.

3. In 2004, a law was passed in France to ban the wearing of religious symbols in state-supported schools. Muslim girls have been expelled for wearing headscarves.

19

When Laws Are Broken

It is easy for us to take our freedoms for granted. Think of some of the things you enjoy about your life: the freedom to choose your own clothes, to ride your bike, to play sports, or even just to meet your friends in the park. These freedoms are your basic rights as a member of society. It is terrible to lose them.

Laws protect our freedoms. Laws also allow society to function in a safe and orderly manner. One consequence of breaking the law is that a person might have his or her own freedom taken away. If a person is found guilty, he or she may be sent to prison or to a juvenile detention center.

What Do You Think ?

When a person goes to prison, he or she is not the only one to suffer. Prisoners' families often break down under the strain of the long absence.

• How do you think the justice system could be fairer to the families of prisoners?

Justifying an Opinion
1. Reread the issue carefully.
2. Try to state both sides of the issue.
3. Review the available evidence.
4. Form and state an opinion.
5. Be prepared to support your opinion with evidence.

A Fair Trial

Taking away a person's liberty is not a small matter. It must be done fairly.

• In the United States, a person is presumed innocent until proven guilty.

• Any person charged with a crime has the right to a trial by **jury**. During the trial, each side of the story is presented to the court by an **attorney**. The jury decides whether the person is guilty.

The Prison Debate

Countries around the world are jailing more and more people. The cost of running prisons gets higher each year. Some people think that there are better ways to prevent crime. They say money should be spent on education to help lift young people out of lives of poverty and crime. In certain cases, there are good alternatives to prison, such as community service and **rehabilitation** programs, which help people not to break the law again.

Yet, many people still believe that prisons make society safer. They argue that the fear of going to prison discourages people from breaking the law.

keeps offenders away from society

2 million people in jail

Prison

hard on families

not the only alternative

getting very expensive

Alternatives to Prison

- **Probation**: Offenders stay in the community and are supervised by a probation officer.

- **Rehabilitation Programs**: Offenders ar sentenced to take part in a treatment program, such as a drug program.

- **Community Service**: Offenders are sentenced to a number of hours working on community projects.

Some states have "three strikes" laws. This means that a person's third crime results in a prison sentence, even if it is only minor. In one case, a man was sentenced to more than 25 years in prison for stealing four cookies! It was his third offense. Some people think this ruling is unjust.

Breaking Laws for a Cause

Sometimes people knowingly refuse to obey laws that they feel are unfair or wrong. This is known as civil disobedience. People who practice civil disobedience are willing to accept the punishment that comes with breaking the law. In this way, they can bring public attention to the situation that they are protesting.

Most acts of civil disobedience are peaceful. Throughout history, many great leaders have paved the way for change through peaceful protests, strikes, marches, and other acts of civil disobedience.

Peaceful Protester

Mohandas Gandhi (1869–1948) was a great Indian leader who fought to free India from British rule. Gandhi believed in "civil disobedience." He told his supporters to peacefully disobey British laws. Gandhi's civil disobedience was a nonviolent way of bringing about change. The protests led to India's independence in 1947.

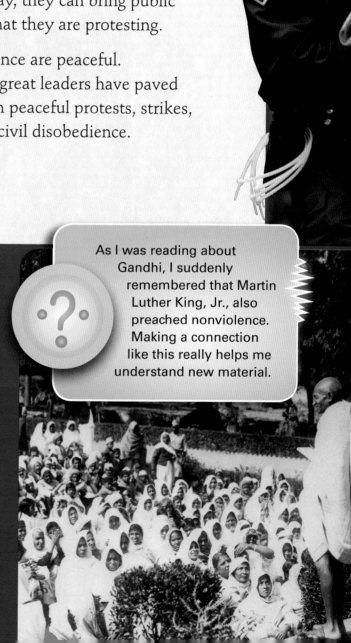

As I was reading about Gandhi, I suddenly remembered that Martin Luther King, Jr., also preached nonviolence. Making a connection like this really helps me understand new material.

What Do You Think ?

Many people believe that civil disobedience is very different from riot, rebellion, and criminal activity. However, even the most peaceful forms of protest can sometimes lead to more violent situations. Some people believe that any kind of lawbreaking can lead people to disrespect other laws in society. They say that unfair situations should be corrected by legal means.

Political Prisoner

From 1948 to the start of the 1990s, South Africa had a system of racial laws called apartheid (*uh PART hite*). Under apartheid, white people had far greater freedom than people of other ethnic groups. Nelson Mandela spent 27 years in prison for opposing apartheid. International pressure finally led to Mandela's release in 1990 and the end of apartheid. He later became President of South Africa.

How Governments Are Organized

In a democracy, we elect our leaders. We can freely criticize the government, practice religion, and choose what groups we join.

Different countries have different political systems. Many of them are not democratic. Some countries have a single ruler that makes most of the decisions. In other countries, personal liberties as we know them are restricted. The needs of the state may be considered more important than those of the individual. Each system places a different importance on personal freedom. As a result, some systems seem more "free" than others.

Democracy

- Democracy is a form of government that began in ancient Greece. The word *democracy* means "rule by the people."
- One of the most important goals of democracy is to protect the liberties, rights, and interests of all citizens.
- Today, many countries around the world are democracies. The people can vote for their leaders.

Monarchy

- Monarchy is a form of government in which a ruler, such as an emperor, a king, a queen, a czar, or a sultan, rules the people for as long as he or she lives.
- Many monarchies today are also democracies. The royal family are important figures, but an elected government leads the country.

What Do You Think ?

People in democracies disagree about what the government's role in society should be. Some people believe basic services, such as sanitation, hospitals, and prisons, are best run by the state. Taxes pay for the services, and everyone has equal access to them.

Others believe taxes are a restriction on people's freedom to choose how to spend their money. They argue that most services should be run by private companies. People then pay only for the services they use.

Totalitarianism

- Totalitarian states are tightly controlled by the government. They allow almost no personal freedom.

- Some totalitarian countries are run by a single **dictator**. The government controls what the media says. It also owns the main businesses.

- In some totalitarian countries, secret police spy on the population, and political enemies are sent to labor camps.

SHOCKER

In some totalitarian countries, such as North Korea, the practice of religion is banned. Simply attending a religious service is a crime punishable by death!

27

Freedoms Fought and Freedoms Won

Liberty did not come cheap. Millions of people fought and died for it in wars and revolutions. Thanks to them, we now have more freedom than our ancestors did. However, the "project" of achieving liberty may never be finished. People continue to stand up for their liberty. New countries are formed. New leaders are elected. In most cases, these hard-won freedoms are a blessing. However, they come with their challenges and responsibilities too.

Modern Milestones of Liberty

Here are some of the modern milestones of freedom.

Milestones is used here to mean "significant events." Milestones were originally stone markers placed along roadsides to indicate distance (in miles) from a town or city.

1776 The Declaration of Independence is signed in America. It recognizes the rights of people to "Life, Liberty and the pursuit of Happiness."

1777 Vermont becomes the first state to outlaw slavery. Slavery was made illegal throughout the United States in 1865.

1917 A **communist** revolution overthrows the Czar of Russia. The Imperial Russian monarchy is replaced by a government based on state ownership of property and shared wealth. However, personal freedoms are soon severely restricted.

1946 An organization of nations is formed. The United Nations works toward world peace. It writes a Universal Declaration of Human Rights.

1964 The United States Civil Rights Act is passed. The Act makes racial discrimination illegal in public life.

1994 South Africa holds its first free and fair elections. The elections mark the end of the system of apartheid in South Africa.

When the Wall Came Tumbling Down

Berlin is the capital city of Germany. A high, heavily guarded wall once separated the eastern and western parts of the city. In many cases, families were separated too. The Berlin Wall was a massive barrier to freedom.
It was built in 1961 to prevent East Germans from crossing into democratic West Germany. In 1989, the East German government collapsed.
The Berlin Wall was knocked down and families were reunited.
People around the world celebrated this victory for liberty.

Many of us enjoy huge freedom of choice when shopping for clothes. It is easy to find good-quality, cheap clothing in stores. However, most clothes are not made in the West. Most are made in developing nations such as China, Bangladesh, or Cambodia. The reason is simple. Wages in these countries are much lower than in the West.

WHAT DO YOU THINK?

Should we be able to buy cheap clothes, regardless of how they are made? Should companies be allowed to mistreat and underpay their workers in order to provide us with low-priced jeans and sneakers?

PRO

I think we should be able to buy cheap clothes. Many people can't afford expensive clothes. Also, clothing factories give jobs to millions of people in poor countries. Those people might lose their jobs if companies had to pay them a higher wage.